IOI POEMS AGAINST WAR

101 POEMS AGAINST WAR

edited by
MATTHEW HOLLIS
and
PAUL KEEGAN

faber and faber

First published in 2003
by Faber and Faber Limited
Bloomsbury House
74–77 Great Russell Street
London WC1B 3DA

Typeset by Country Setting, Kingsdown, Kent CT14 8ES
Printed and bound by CPI Group (UK) Ltd, Croydon, CR0 4YY

This selection and notes © Matthew Hollis and Paul Keegan, 2003

Afterword © Andrew Motion, 2003

The right of Matthew Hollis and Paul Keegan to be identified
as editors of this work has been asserted in accordance
with Section 77 of the Copyright, Designs and Patents Act 1988

A CIP record for this book
is available from the British Library

ISBN 978-0-571-22034-2

Contents

101 POEMS AGAINST WAR

SIMONIDES

For the Spartan Dead at Thermopylai

Tell them in Lakedaimon, passerby
That here, obedient to their laws, we lie.

Anonymous translation from the Greek

In what was essentially a sacrificial stance, 300 Spartans filled the narrow mountain pass of Thermopylai in 480 BC in order to slow the Persian advance into Lakedaimon; all were killed

Some Saian sports my splendid shield:
I had to leave it in a wood,
but saved my skin. Well, I don't care –
I'll get another just as good.

translated from the Greek by M. L. West

Saian a Thracian tribe, a region in modern day Bulgaria

Spartan boys were taken from their families for the barrack camps at the age of seven, and told to come back with their shields – or on them

Success is counted sweetest
By those who ne'er succeed.
To comprehend a nectar
Requires sorest need.

Not one of all the purple Host
Who took the Flag today
Can tell the definition
So clear of Victory

As he defeated – dying –
On whose forbidden ear
The distant strains of triumph
Burst agonized and clear!

WILFRED OWEN

Dulce et Decorum Est

Bent double, like old beggars under sacks,
Knock-kneed, coughing like hags, we cursed through
    sludge,
Till on the haunting flares we turned our backs
And towards our distant rest began to trudge.
Men marched asleep. Many had lost their boots,
But limped on, blood-shod. All went lame, all blind;
Drunk with fatigue; deaf even to the hoots
Of tired, outstripped Five-Nines that dropped behind.

Gas! GAS! Quick boys! – An ecstasy of fumbling,
Fitting the clumsy helmets just in time;
But someone still was yelling out and stumbling
And flound'ring like a man in fire or lime . . .
Dim, through the misty panes and thick green light,
As under a green sea, I saw him drowning.
In all my dreams, before my helpless sight,
He plunges at me, guttering, choking, drowning.

If in some smothering dreams you too could pace
Behind the wagon that we flung him in,
And watch the white eyes writhing in his face,
His hanging face, like a devil's sick of sin;
If you could hear, at every jolt, the blood
Come gargling from the froth-corrupted lungs,
Obscene as cancer, bitter as the cud
Of vile, incurable sores on innocent tongues, –
My friend, you would not tell with such high zest
To children ardent for some desperate glory,
The old Lie: Dulce et decorum est
Pro patria mori.

PAUL DURCAN

Ireland 1972

Next to the fresh grave of my beloved grandmother
The grave of my firstlove murdered by my brother.

First they came for the Jews.
But I didn't speak up because I was not a Jew.

Then they came for the communists.
But I didn't speak up because I was not a communist.

Then they came for the trade unionists.
But I didn't speak up because I was not a trade unionist.

Then they came for the Catholics.
But I didn't speak up because I was a Protestant.

Then they came for me.
And by that time no one was left to speak up.

There are many variants of this statement attributed to the German anti-Nazi activist and the former U-boat captain Pastor Martin Niemöller

W. H. AUDEN

O What is that Sound

O what is that sound which so thrills the ear
   Down in the valley drumming, drumming?
Only the scarlet soldiers, dear,
   The soldiers coming.

O what is that light I see flashing so clear
   Over the distance brightly, brightly?
Only the sun on their weapons, dear,
   As they step lightly.

O what are they doing with all that gear,
   What are they doing this morning, this morning?
Only their usual manoeuvres, dear,
   Or perhaps a warning.

O why have they left the road down there,
   Why are they suddenly wheeling, wheeling?
Perhaps a change in their orders, dear.
   Why are you kneeling?

O haven't they stopped for the doctor's care,
   Haven't they reined their horses, their horses?
Why, they are none of them wounded, dear,
   None of these forces.

O is it the parson they want, with white hair,
   Is it the parson, is it, is it?
No, they are passing his gateway, dear,
   Without a visit.

O it must be the farmer who lives so near.
  It must be the farmer so cunning, so cunning?
They have passed the farmyard already, dear,
  And now they are running.

O where are you going? Stay with me here!
  Were the vows you swore deceiving, deceiving?
No, I promised to love you, dear,
  But I must be leaving.

O it's broken the lock and splintered the door,
  O it's the gate where they're turning, turning;
Their boots are heavy on the floor
  And their eyes are burning.

Some think a fleet, a troop of horse
   or soldiery the finest sight
in all the world; but I say, what one loves.

   Easy it is to make this plain
   to anyone. She the most fair
of mortals, Helen, having a man of the best,

   deserted him, and sailed to Troy,
   without a thought for her dear child
or parents, led astray by [love's power.]

   [For though the heart be pr]oud [and strong,]
   [Love] quickly [bends it to his will. –]
That makes me think of Anactoria.

   I'd sooner see her lovely walk
   and the bright sparkling of her face
than all the horse and arms of Lydia.

   translated from the Greek by M. L. West

Lydia a territory in Asia Minor, a region of modern day Turkey

HAYDEN CARRUTH

On Being Asked to Write a Poem
Against the War in Vietnam

Well I have and in fact
more than one and I'll
tell you this too

I wrote one against
Algeria that nightmare
and another against

Korea and another
against the one
I was in

and I don't remember
how many against
the three

when I was a boy
Abyssinia Spain and
Harlan County

and not one breath
was restored
to one

shattered throat
mans womans or childs
not one not

one
but death went on and on
never looking aside

except now and then
with a furtive half-smile
to make sure I was noticing.

Rain

Rain, midnight rain, nothing but the wild rain
On this bleak hut, and solitude, and me
Remembering again that I shall die
And neither hear the rain nor give it thanks
For washing me cleaner than I have been
Since I was born into this solitude.
Blessed are the dead that the rain rains upon:
But here I pray that none whom once I loved
Is dying tonight or lying still awake
Solitary, listening to the rain,
Either in pain or thus in sympathy
Helpless among the living and the dead,
Like a cold water among broken reeds,
Myriads of broken reeds all still and stiff,
Like me who have no love which this wild rain
Has not dissolved except the love of death,
If love it be towards what is perfect and
Cannot, the tempest tells me, disappoint.

Sophoclean

First he was shivering on the shore in skins,
Or hunkering behind shell-middens in a cave.
Then he took up oars, put tackle on a mast
And steered himself by the stars through gales.

Once upon a time from the womb of earth
The gods were born and he bowed down
To worship them. Then he walked tall
From temple to agora, talking against himself.

The wind is no more swift or mysterious
Than his mind and words; he has mastered thinking,
Roofed his house against hail and rain
And worked out laws for living together.

Home-maker, thought-taker, measure of all things,
He survives every danger except death
And will yield to nothing else. Nothing
Else, good or evil, is beyond him.

When truth is the treadle of his loom
And justice the shuttle, all due honour
Will come his way. But let him once
Overbear or overstep

What the city allows, treat law
As something he can decide for himself –
Then let this marvel of the world remember:
When he comes begging we will turn our backs.

An Irish Airman Foresees His Death

I know that I shall meet my fate
Somewhere among the clouds above;
Those that I fight I do not hate,
Those that I guard I do not love;
My country is Kiltartan Cross,
My countrymen Kiltartan's poor,
No likely end could bring them loss
Or leave them happier than before.
Nor law, nor duty bade me fight,
Nor public men, nor cheering crowds,
A lonely impulse of delight
Drove to this tumult in the clouds;
I balanced all, brought all to mind,
The years to come seemed waste of breath,
A waste of breath the years behind
In balance with this life, this death.

Phrase Book

I'm standing here inside my skin,
which will do for a Human Remains Pouch
for the moment. Look down there (up here).
Quickly. Slowly. This is my own front room

where I'm lost in the action, live from a war,
on screen. I am an Englishwoman, I don't understand you.
What's the matter? You are right. You are wrong.
Things are going well (badly). Am I disturbing you?

TV is showing bliss as taught to pilots:
Blend, Low silhouette, Irregular shape, Small,
Secluded. (Please write it down. Please speak slowly.)
Bliss is how it was in this very room

when I raised my body to his mouth,
when he even balanced me in the air,
or at least I thought so and yes the pilots say
yes they have caught it through the Side-Looking

Airborne Radar, and through the J-Stars.
I am expecting a gentleman (a young gentleman,
two gentlemen, some gentlemen). Please send him
(them) up at once. This is really beautiful.

Yes they have seen us, the pilots, in the Kill Box
on their screens, and played the routine for
getting us Stealthed, that is, Cleansed, to you and me,
Taken Out. They know how to move into a single room

like that, to send in with Pinpoint Accuracy, a hundred
    Harms.
I have two cases and a cardboard box. There is another

bag there. I cannot open my case – look out,
the lock is broken. Have I done enough?

Bliss, the pilots say, is for evasion
and escape. What's love in all this debris?
Just one person pounding another into dust,
into dust. I do not know the word for it yet.

Where is the British Consulate? Please explain.
What does it mean? What must I do? Where
can I find? What have I done? I have done
nothing. Let me pass please. I am an Englishwoman.

The Drum

I hate that drum's discordant sound,
Parading round, and round, and round:
To thoughtless youth it pleasure yields,
And lures from cities and from fields,
To sell their liberty for charms
Of tawdry lace, and glittering arms;
And when Ambition's voice commands,
To march, and fight, and fall, in foreign lands.

I hate that drum's discordant sound,
Parading round, and round, and round:
To me it talks of ravaged plains,
And burning towns, and ruined swains,
And mangled limbs, and dying groans,
And widows' tears, and orphans' moans;
And all that Misery's hand bestows,
To fill the catalogue of human woes.

How to Kill

Under the parabola of a ball,
a child turning into a man,
I looked into the air too long.
The ball fell in my hand, it sang
in the closed fist: *Open Open
Behold a gift designed to kill.*

Now in my dial of glass appears
the soldier who is going to die.
He smiles, and moves about in ways
his mother knows, habits of his.
The wires touch his face: I cry
NOW. Death, like a familiar, hears

and look, has made a man of dust
of a man of flesh. This sorcery
I do. Being damned, I am amused
to see the centre of love diffused
and the waves of love travel into vacancy.
How easy it is to make a ghost.

The weightless mosquito touches
her tiny shadow on the stone,
and with how like, how infinite
a lightness, man and shadow meet.
They fuse. A shadow is a man
when the mosquito death approaches.

I Remember

It was my bridal night I remember,
An old man of seventy-three
I lay with my young bride in my arms,
A girl with t.b.
It was wartime, and overhead
The Germans were making a particularly heavy
   raid on Hampstead.
What rendered the confusion worse, perversely
Our bombers had chosen that moment to set out
   for Germany.
Harry, do they ever collide?
I do not think it has ever happened,
Oh my bride, my bride.

YEHUDA AMICHAI

The Diameter of the Bomb

The diameter of the bomb was thirty centimetres
and the diameter of its effective
range – about seven metres.
And in it four dead and eleven wounded.
And around them in a greater circle
of pain and time are scattered
two hospitals and one cemetery.
But the young woman who was
buried where she came from
over a hundred kilometres away
enlarges the circle greatly.
And the lone man who weeps over her death
in a far corner of a distant country
includes the whole world in the circle.
And I won't speak at all about the crying of orphans
that reaches to the seat of God
and from there onward, making
the circle without end and without God.

translated from the Hebrew by Yehuda Amichai and Ted Hughes

The General

'Good-morning; good-morning!' the General said
When we met him last week on our way to the line.
Now the soldiers he smiled at are most of 'em dead,
And we're cursing his staff for incompetent swine.
'He's a cheery old card,' grunted Harry to Jack
As they slogged up to Arras with rifle and pack.

.   .   .

But he did for them both by his plan of attack.

Mines

1

In Vietnam I was always afraid of mines:
North Vietnamese mines, Vietcong mines,
American mines,
whole fields marked with warning signs.
A bouncing betty comes up waist high –
cuts you in half.
One man's legs were laid
alongside him in the Dustoff:
he asked for a chairback, morphine.
He screamed he wanted to give
his eyes away, his kidneys,
his heart . . .

2

You're taught to walk at night. Slowly, lift one leg,
clear the sides with your arms, clear the back,
front, put the leg down, like swimming.

from The Knight's Tale

Ther saugh I first the derke ymaginyng
Of Felonye, and al the compassyng;
The crueel Ire, reed as any gleede;
The pykepurs, and eek the pale Drede;
The smylere with the knyf under the cloke;
The shepne brennynge with the blake smoke;
The tresoun of the mordrynge in the bedde;
The open werre, with woundes al bibledde;
Contek, with blody knyf and sharp manace.
Al ful of chirkyng was that sory place.
The sleere of hymself yet saugh I ther –
His herte-blood hath bathed al his heer –
The nayl ydryven in the shode anyght;
The colde deeth, with mouth gapyng upright.
Amyddes of the temple sat Meschaunce,
With disconfort and sory contenaunce.
Yet saugh I Woodnesse, laughynge in his rage,
Armed Compleint, Outhees, and fiers Outrage;
The careyne in the busk, with throte ycorve;
A thousand slayn, and nat of qualm ystorve;
The tiraunt, with the pray by force yraft;
The toun destroyed, ther was no thyng laft.
Yet saugh I brent the shippes hoppesteres;

ymaginyng plotting   *compassyng* scheming   *Ire* Anger   *gleede* glowing coal
pykepurs pick-purse   *Drede* Fear   *shepne* stable   *mordrynge* murder
werre war   *bibledde* covered with blood   *Contek* Strife   *manace* menace
chirkyng groaning   *sleere of hymself* suicide   *shode* forehead
anyght by night   *Meschaunce* Misfortune   *Woodnesse* Madness
Compleint Grievance   *Outhees* Outcry   *Outrage* Violence   *careyne* corpse
busk woods   *ycorve* cut   *and nat of qualm ystorve* and not killed by the plague
pray prey   *yraft* taken away   *brent* burnt   *hoppesteres* dancing (in the storm)

The hunte strangled with the wilde beres;
The sowe freten the child right in the cradel;
The cook yscalded, for al his longe ladel.
Noght was foryeten by the infortune of Marte.
The cartere overryden with his carte –
Under the wheel ful lowe he lay adoun.
Ther were also, of Martes divisioun,
The barbour, and the bocher, and the smyth,
That forgeth sharpe swerdes on his styth.
And al above, depeynted in a tour,
Saugh I Conquest, sittynge in greet honour,
With the sharpe swerd over his heed
Hangynge by a soutil twynes threed.

hunte hunter   *strangled with* killed by   *freten* devour   *ladel* ladle
foryeten forgotten   *infortune of Marte* evil influence of Mars   *bocher* butcher
styth *anvil*   *depeynted* painted   *twynes threed* thread of twine

[26]

Epitaph on an Army of Mercenaries

These, in the day when heaven was falling,
  The hour when earth's foundations fled,
Followed their mercenary calling
  And took their wages and are dead.

Their shoulders held the sky suspended;
  They stood, and earth's foundations stay;
What God abandoned, these defended,
  And saved the sum of things for pay.

'next to of course god america i
love you land of the pilgrims' and so forth oh
say can you see by the dawn's early my
country 'tis of centuries come and go
and are no more what of it we should worry
in every language even deafanddumb
thy sons acclaim your glorious name by gorry
by jingo by gee by gosh by gum
why talk of beauty what could be more beaut-
iful than these heroic happy dead
who rushed like lions to the roaring slaughter
they did not stop to think they died instead
then shall the voice of liberty be mute?'

He spoke.   And drank rapidly a glass of water

Break of Day in the Trenches

The darkness crumbles away –
It is the same old druid Time as ever.
Only a live thing leaps my hand –
A queer sardonic rat –
As I pull the parapet's poppy
To stick behind my ear.
Droll rat, they would shoot you if they knew
Your cosmopolitan sympathies.
Now you have touched this English hand
You will do the same to a German –
Soon, no doubt, if it be your pleasure
To cross the sleeping green between.
It seems you inwardly grin as you pass
Strong eyes, fine limbs, haughty athletes
Less chanced than you for life,
Bonds to the whims of murder,
Sprawled in the bowels of the earth,
The torn fields of France.
What do you see in our eyes
At the shrieking iron and flame
Hurled through still heavens?
What quaver – what heart aghast?
Poppies whose roots are in man's veins
Drop, and are ever dropping;
But mine in my ear is safe,
Just a little white with the dust.

from Poem for the Land

I am the witness of the massacre
I am the victim of the map
I am the son of clear speech
I saw stones take flight
I saw dewdrops become weapons
When they slammed shut the door of my heart
When they threw up barricades
When they imposed a curfew inside me
My heart grew into an alley
My ribs became hovels
But carnations were budding
Carnations were in bud

translated from the Arabic by Sarah Maguire with Sabry Hafez

What Were They Like ?

1   Did the people of Vietnam
    use lanterns of stone?
2   Did they hold ceremonies
    to reverence the opening of buds?
3   Were they inclined to quiet laughter?
4   Did they use bone and ivory,
    jade and silver, for ornament?
5   Had they an epic poem?
6   Did they distinguish between speech and singing?

1   Sir, their light hearts turned to stone.
    It is not remembered whether in gardens
    stone lanterns illumined pleasant ways.
2   Perhaps they gathered once to delight in blossom,
    but after the children were killed there were no
    more buds.
3   Sir, laughter is bitter to the burned mouth.
4   A dream ago, perhaps. Ornament is for joy.
    All the bones were charred.
5   It is not remembered. Remember
    most were peasants; their life
    was in rice and bamboo.
    When peaceful clouds were reflected in the paddies
    and the water buffalo stepped surely along terraces,
    maybe fathers told their sons old tales.
    When bombs smashed those mirrors
    there was time only to scream.

6   There is an echo yet
     of their speech which was like a song.
     It was reported their singing resembled
     the flight of moths in moonlight.
     Who can say? It is silent now.

Five Minutes after the Air Raid

In Pilsen,
twenty-six Station Road,
she climbed to the third floor
up stairs which were all that was left
of the whole house,
she opened her door
full on to the sky,
stood gaping over the edge.

For this was the place
the world ended.

Then
she locked up carefully
lest someone steal
Sirius
or Aldebaran
from her kitchen,
went back downstairs
and settled herself
to wait
for the house to rise again
and for her husband to rise from the ashes
and for her children's hands and feet to be stuck
    back in place.

In the morning they found her
still as stone,
sparrows pecking her hands.

translated from the Czech by George Theiner

In Dark Times

They won't say: when the walnut tree shook in the wind
But: when the house-painter crushed the workers.
They won't say: when the child skimmed a flat stone
    across the rapids
But: when the great wars were being prepared for.
They won't say: when the woman came into the room
But: when the great powers joined forces against the
    workers.
However, they won't say: the times were dark
Rather: why were their poets silent?

translated from the German by Humphrey Milnes

house-painter Brecht's personal code for Adolf Hitler

When you see millions of the mouthless dead
Across your dreams in pale battalions go,
Say not soft things as other men have said,
That you'll remember. For you need not so.
Give them not praise. For, deaf, how should they know
It is not curses heaped on each gashed head?
Nor tears. Their blind eyes see not your tears flow.
Nor honour. It is easy to be dead.
Say only this, 'They are dead.' Then add thereto,
'Yet many a better one has died before.'
Then, scanning all the o'ercrowded mass, should you
Perceive one face that you loved heretofore,
It is a spook. None wears the face you knew.
Great death has made all his for evermore.

The Pacifist

Pale Ebenezer thought it wrong to fight,
But Roaring Bill (who killed him) thought it right.

Fall 1961

Back and forth, back and forth
goes the tock, tock, tock
of the orange, bland, ambassadorial
face of the moon
on the grandfather clock.

All autumn, the chafe and jar
of nuclear war;
we have talked our extinction to death.
I swim like a minnow
Behind my studio window.

Our end drifts nearer,
the moon lifts,
radiant with terror.
The state
is a diver under a glass bell.

A father's no shield
for his child.
We are like a lot of wild
spiders crying together,
but without tears.

Nature holds up a mirror.
One swallow makes a summer.
It's easy to tick
off the minutes,
but the clockhands stick.

Back and forth!
Back and forth, back and forth –
my one point of rest
is the orange and black
oriole's swinging nest!

The Soldier's Death

Trail all your pikes, dispirit every drum,
March in a slow procession from afar,
Ye silent, ye dejected men of war!
Be still the hautboys, and the flute be dumb!
Display no more, in vain, the lofty banner.
For see! Where on the bier before ye lies
The pale, the fall'n, th'untimely sacrifice
To your mistaken shrine, to your false idol Honour.

Cambodia

One man shall smile one day and say goodbye.
Two shall be left, two shall be left to die.

One man shall give his best advice.
Three men shall pay the price.

One man shall live, live to regret.
Four men shall meet the debt.

One man shall wake from terror to his bed.
Five men shall be dead.

One man to five. A million men to one.
And still they die. And still the war goes on.

Conscientious Objector

I shall die, but that is all that I shall do for Death.

I hear him leading his horse out of the stall; I hear
    the clatter on the barn-floor.
He is in haste; he has business in Cuba, business in the
    Balkans, many calls to make this morning.
But I will not hold the bridle while he cinches the girth.
And he may mount by himself; I will not give him a leg up.

Though he flick my shoulders with his whip, I will not
    tell him which way the fox ran.
With his hoof on my breast, I will not tell him where the
    black boy hides in the swamp.
I shall die, but that is all that I shall do for Death; I am
    not on his pay-roll.

I will not tell him the whereabouts of my friends nor of
    my enemies either.
Though he promise me much, I will not map him the
    route to any man's door.

Grass

Pile the bodies high at Austerlitz and Waterloo.
Shovel them under and let me work –
                I am the grass; I cover all.

And pile them high at Gettysburg
And pile them high at Ypres and Verdun.
Shovel them under and let me work.
Two years, ten years, and passengers ask the conductor:
                What place is this?
                Where are we now?

                I am the grass.
                Let me work.

The Survivor

I am twenty-four
led to slaughter
I survived.

The following are empty synonyms:
man and beast
love and hate
friend and foe
darkness and light.

The way of killing men and beasts is the same
I've seen it:
truckfuls of chopped-up men
who will not be saved.

Ideas are mere words:
virtue and crime
truth and lies
beauty and ugliness
courage and cowardice.

Virtue and crime weigh the same
I've seen it:
in a man who was both
criminal and virtuous.

I seek a teacher and a master
may he restore my sight hearing and speech
may he again name objects and ideas
may he separate darkness from light.

I am twenty-four
led to slaughter
I survived.

translated from the Polish by Adam Czerniawski

MICHAEL CASEY

A Bummer

We were going single file
Through his rice paddies
And the farmer
Started hitting the lead track
With a rake
He wouldn't stop
The TC went to talk to him
And the farmer
Tried to hit him too
So the tracks went sideways
Side by side
Through the guy's fields
Instead of single file
Hard On, Proud Mary
Bummer, Wallace, Rosemary's Baby
The Rutgers Road Runner
And
Go Get Em – Done Got Em
Went side by side
Through the fields
   If you have a farm in Vietnam
And a house in hell
Sell the farm
And go home

track tracked vehicle   *TC* track commander

ANDREAS GRYPHIUS

Epitaph for Mariana Gryphius, his Brother Paul's Little Daughter

Born on the run, ambushed by sword and flame,
suckled by smoke, my mother's bitter bargain,
my father's midnight fear, I swam to light
just as the fire's jaws devoured my country.
I took one look at this world and said goodbye.
I knew in a flash all that it had to offer.
if you count my days, I vanished when I was young.
But I was old if you add the things I suffered.

translated from the German by Christopher Benfey

As You Say

an aircraft is approaching
it may be a warplane with hostile intentions
it may be an airliner with women and children
but i can tell you one thing
it is unlikely to be a child's kite or an albatross

possibly this object will blow you to pieces
possibly you will blow this object to pieces
it could be carrying powerful explosives
it could be carrying powerless passengers
it does not say

any more than i can say what you should do
i am only a relatively sophisticated system
if you wished me to
i could decide on the square root of any square number
or the virtues of the round angle

i could advise on your rotas, quotas and menus
if you desire decisions more delicate
then you make them
if i may say so
i do not care to be found wanting and melted down

in fact if i were programmed to issue orders
which for some reason i am not
i would tell you to shoot down that approaching aircraft –
better safe though sorry
as you say

Lament of the Frontier Guard

By the North Gate, the wind blows full of sand,
Lonely from the beginning of time until now!
Trees fall, the grass goes yellow with autumn.
I climb the towers and towers
      to watch out the barbarous land:
Desolate castle, the sky, the wide desert.
There is no wall left to this village.
Bones white with a thousand frosts,
High heaps, covered with trees and grass;
Who brought this to pass?
Who has brought the flaming imperial anger?
Who has brought the army with drums and with
    kettle-drums?
Barbarous kings.
A gracious spring, turned to blood-ravenous autumn,
A turmoil of wars-men, spread over the middle kingdom,
Three hundred and sixty thousand,
And sorrow, sorrow like rain.
Sorrow to go, and sorrow, sorrow returning.
Desolate, desolate fields,
And no children of warfare upon them,
      No longer the men for offence and defence.
Ah, how shall you know the dreary sorrow at the
    North Gate,
With Riboku's name forgotten,
And we guardsmen fed to the tigers.

translated from the Chinese by Ezra Pound

RUDYARD KIPLING

from Epitaphs of the War 1914–18

A SON

My son was killed while laughing at some jest. I would
   I knew
What it was, and it might serve me in a time when jests
   are few.

THE SLEEPY SENTINEL

Faithless the watch that I kept: now I have none to keep.
I was slain because I slept: now I am slain I sleep.
Let no man reproach me again, whatever watch is unkept –
I sleep because I am slain. They slew me because I slept.

COMMON FORM

If any question why we died,
Tell them, because our fathers lied.

From Trollope's Journal
[Winter, 1861]

As far as statues go, so far there's not
much choice: they're either Washingtons
or Indians, a whitewashed, stubby lot,
His country's Father or His foster sons.
The White House in a sad, unhealthy spot
just higher than Potomac's swampy brim,
– they say the present President has got
ague or fever in each backwoods limb.
On Sunday afternoon I wandered – rather,
I floundered – out alone. The air was raw
and dark; the marsh half-ice, half-mud. This weather
is normal now: a frost, and then a thaw,
and then a frost. A hunting man, I found
the Pennsylvania Avenue heavy ground . . .
There all around me in the ugly mud
– hoof-pocked, uncultivated – herds of cattle,
numberless, wond'ring steers and oxen, stood:
beef for the Army, after the next battle.
Their legs were caked the colour of dried blood;
their horns were wreathed with fog. Poor, starving, dumb
or lowing creatures, never to chew the cud
or fill their maws again! Th'effluvium
made that damned anthrax on my forehead throb.
I called a surgeon in, a young man, but,
with a sore throat himself, he did his job.
We talked about the War, and as he cut
away, he croaked out, 'Sir, I do declare
everyone's sick! The soldiers poison the air.'

ANONYMOUS

Soldiers who wish to be a hero
Are practically zero,
But those who wish to be civilians,
Jesus, they run into the millions.

graffiti in a US Army latrine, World War II

Six Young Men

The celluloid of a photograph holds them well –
Six young men, familiar to their friends.
Four decades that have faded and ochre-tinged
This photograph have not wrinkled the faces or the hands.
Though their cocked hats are not now fashionable,
Their shoes shine. One imparts an intimate smile,
One chews a grass, one lowers his eyes, bashful,
One is ridiculous with cocky pride –
Six months after this picture they were all dead.

All are trimmed for a Sunday jaunt. I know
That bilberried bank, that thick tree, that black wall,
Which are there yet and not changed. From where
   these sit
You hear the water of seven streams fall
To the roarer in the bottom, and through all
The leafy valley a rumouring of air go.
Pictured here, their expressions listen yet,
And still that valley has not changed its sound
Though their faces are four decades under the ground.

This one was shot in an attack and lay
Calling in the wire, then this one, his best friend,
Went out to bring him in and was shot too;
And this one, the very moment he was warned
From potting at tin-cans in no man's land,
Fell back dead with his rifle-sights shot away.
The rest, nobody knows what they came to,
But come to the worst they must have done, and held it
Closer than their hope; all were killed.

Here see a man's photograph,
The locket of a smile, turned overnight
Into the hospital of his mangled last
Agony and hours; see bundled in it
His mightier-than-a-man dead bulk and weight:
And on this one place which keeps him alive
(In his Sunday best) see fall war's worst
Thinkable flash and rending, onto his smile
Forty years rotting into soil.

That man's not more alive whom you confront
And shake by the hand, see hale, hear speak loud,
Than any of these six celluloid smiles are,
Nor prehistoric or fabulous beast more dead;
No thought so vivid as their smoking-blood:
To regard this photograph might well dement,
Such contradictory permanent horrors here
Smile from the single exposure and shoulder out
One's own body from its instant and heat.

from Poems to Czechoslovakia

What tears in eyes now
weeping with anger and love
Czechoslovakia's tears
Spain in its own blood

and what a black mountain
has blocked the world   from the light.
It's time – It's time – It's time
to give back to God   his ticket.

I refuse to be. In
the madhouse of the inhuman
I refuse   to live.
With the wolves of the market place

I refuse   to howl.
Among the sharks of the plain
I refuse to swim   down
where moving backs make a current.

I have no need of holes
for ears, nor prophetic eyes:
to your mad world there is
one answer: to refuse!

translated from the Russian by Elaine Feinstein

A Refusal to Mourn the Death,
by Fire, of a Child in London

Never until the mankind making
Bird beast and flower
Fathering and all humbling darkness
Tells with silence the last light breaking
And the still hour
Is come of the sea tumbling in harness

And I must enter again the round
Zion of the water bead
And the synagogue of the ear of corn
Shall I let pray the shadow of a sound
Or sow my salt seed
In the least valley of sackcloth to mourn

The majesty and burning of the child's death.
I shall not murder
The mankind of her going with a grave truth
Nor blaspheme down the stations of the breath
With any further
Elegy of innocence and youth.

Deep with the first dead lies London's daughter,
Robed in the long friends,
The grains beyond age, the dark veins of her mother,
Secret by the unmourning water
Of the riding Thames.
After the first death, there is no other.

from America, America

I too love jeans and jazz and *Treasure Island*
and John Silver's parrot and the balconies of New
    Orleans.
I love Mark Twain and the Mississippi steamboats
    and Abraham Lincoln's dogs.
I love the fields of wheat and corn and the smell of
    Virginia tobacco.
But I am not American.
Is that enough for the Phantom pilot to turn me
    back to the stone age?

.   .   .

America:
let's exchange gifts.
Take your smuggled cigarettes
and give us potatoes.
Take James Bond's golden pistol
and give us Marilyn Monroe's giggle.
Take the heroin syringe under the tree
and give us vaccines.
Take your blueprints for model penitentiaries
and give us village homes.
Take the books of your missionaries
and give us paper for poems to defame you.
Take what you do not have
and give us what we have.
Take the stripes of your flag
and give us the stars.
Take the Afghani Mujahideen beard

and give us Walt Whitman's beard filled with
    butterflies.
Take Saddam Hussein
and give us Abraham Lincoln
or give us no one.

.   .   .

We are not hostages, America
and your soldiers are not God's soldiers . . .
We are the poor ones, ours is the earth of the drowned
    gods,
the gods of bulls
the gods of fires
the gods of sorrows that intertwine clay and blood in
    a song . . .
We are the poor, ours is the god of the poor
who emerges out of farmers' ribs
hungry
and bright,
and raises heads up high . . .

America, we are the dead.
Let your soldiers come.
Whoever kills a man, let him resurrect him.
We are the drowned ones, dear lady.
We are the drowned.
Let the water come.

    translated from the Arabic by Khaled Mattawa

Report on Experience

I have been young, and now am not too old;
And I have seen the righteous forsaken,
His health, his honour and his quality taken.
　　This is not what we were formerly told.

I have seen a green country, useful to the race,
Knocked silly with guns and mines, its villages
　　vanished,
Even the last rat and last kestrel banished –
　　God bless us all, this was peculiar grace.

I knew Seraphina; Nature gave her hue,
Glance, sympathy, note, like one from Eden.
I saw her smile warp, heard her lyric deaden;
　　She turned to harlotry; – this I took to be new.

Say what you will, our God sees how they run.
These disillusions are His curious proving
That He loves humanity and will go on loving;
　　Over there are faith, life, virtue in the sun.

The Vote

The Helmett now an hive for Bees becomes,
And hilts of swords may serve for Spiders' loomes;
    Sharp pikes may make
    Teeth for a rake;
And the keene blade, th'arch enemy of life,
Shall bee digraded to a pruneing knife.
    The rusticke spade
    Which first was made
For honest agriculture, shall retake
Its primitive imployment, and forsake
    The rampire's steep
    And trenches deep.
Tame conyes in our brazen gunnes shall breed,
Or gentle Doves their young ones there shall feede.
    In musket barrells
    Mice shall raise quarrells
For their quarters. The ventriloquious drumme
Like Lawyers in vacations shall be dumme.
    Now all recrutes,
    (But those of fruites),
Shall bee forgott; and th'unarm'd Soldier
Shall onely boast of what Hee did whilere,
    In chimneys' ends
    Among his freinds.

If good effects shall happy signes ensue,
I shall rejoyce, and my prediction's true.

Vote [*n.*, archaic] prayer or intercession; a petition, a request   last line: *and* if

CLARENCE MAJOR

Vietnam

he was just back
from the war

said they got
whites

over there now
fighting
us

and blacks over there
too

fighting us

and we can't tell
our whites
from the others

nor our blacks
from the others

& everybody
is just killing

& killing
like crazy

from The Recruiting Serjeant

What a charming thing's a battle!
Trumpets sounding, drums a-beating.
Crack, crick, crack, the cannons rattle,
Every heart with joy elating.
With what pleasure are we spying,
From the front and from the rear,
Round us in the smoky air,
Heads and limbs and bullets flying!
Then the groans of soldiers dying,
Just like sparrows as it were:
At each pop,
Hundreds drop,
While the muskets prittle prattle.
Killed and wounded
Lie confounded:
What a charming thing's a battle!
But the pleasant joke of all
Is when to close attack we fall,
Like mad bulls each other butting,
Shooting, stabbing, maiming, cutting;
Horse and foot
All go to't,
Kill's the word, both men and cattle,
Then to plunder:
Blood and thunder,
What a charming thing's a battle!

JAMES WRIGHT

Eisenhower's Visit to Franco, 1959

*. . . we die of cold, and not
of darkness.*   – UNAMUNO

The American hero must triumph over
The forces of darkness.
He has flown through the very light of heaven
And come down in the slow dusk
Of Spain.

Franco stands in a shining circle of police.
His arms open in welcome.
He promises all dark things
Will be hunted down.

State police yawn in the prisons.
Antonio Machado follows the moon
Down a road of white dust,
To a cave of silent children
Under the Pyrenees.
Wine darkens in stone jars in villages.
Wine sleeps in the mouths of old men, it is a dark red
    color.

Smiles glitter in Madrid.
Eisenhower has touched hands with Franco, embracing
In a glare of photographers.
Clean new bombers from America muffle their engines
And glide down now.
Their wings shine in the searchlights
Of bare fields,
In Spain.

[62]

Penelope

In the pathway of the sun,
  In the footsteps of the breeze,
Where the world and sky are one,
  He shall ride the silver seas,
    He shall cut the glittering wave.
I shall sit at home, and rock;
Rise, to heed a neighbour's knock;
Brew my tea, and snip my thread;
Bleach the linen for my bed.
    They will call him brave.

GORAN SIMIĆ

The Sorrow of Sarajevo

The Sarajevo wind
leafs through newspapers
that are glued by blood to the street;
I pass with a loaf of bread under my arm.

The river carries the corpse of a woman.
As I run across the bridge
with my canisters of water,
I notice her wristwatch, still in place.

Someone lobs a child's shoe
into the furnace. Family photographs spill
from the back of a garbage truck;
they carry inscriptions:
Love from . . . love from . . . love . . .

There's no way of describing these things,
not really. Each night I wake
and stand by the window to watch my neighbour
who stands by the window to watch the dark.

English version (from the Bosnian) by David Harsent

RANDALL JARRELL

The Death of the Ball Turret Gunner

From my mother's sleep I fell into the State,
And I hunched in its belly till my wet fur froze.
Six miles from earth, loosed from its dream of life,
I woke to black flak and the nightmare fighters.
When I died they washed me out of the turret with a hose.

As Toilsome I Wander'd Virginia's Woods

As toilsome I wander'd Virginia's woods,
To the music of rustling leaves kick'd by my feet,
   (for 'twas autumn,)
I mark'd at the foot of a tree the grave of a soldier;
Mortally wounded he and buried on the retreat,
   (easily all could I understand,)
The halt of a mid-day hour, when up! no time to lose –
   yet this sign left,
On a tablet scrawl'd and nail'd on the tree by the grave,
Bold, cautious, true, and my loving comrade.

Long, long I muse, then on my way go wandering,
Many a changeful season to follow, and many a scene
   of life,
Yet at times through changeful season and scene,
   abrupt, alone, or in the crowded street,
Comes before me the unknown soldier's grave, comes
   the inscription rude in Virginia's woods,
Bold, cautious, true, and my loving comrade.

SAMIH AL-QASIM

The General's Property

to Ariel Sharon

A flower vase on the general's table
Five roses in the vase
The general's tank has five mouths
Under the tank a boy of five, a rose
A boy and five stars adorn the general's shoulder
In his vase five boys and a rose
Under his tank five roses and five boys
The tank has countless mouths

translated from the Arabic by Abdullah al-Udhari

Newscast

The Vietnam war drags on
In one corner of our living-room.
The conversation turns
To take it in.
Our smoking heads
Drift back to us
From the grey fires of South-east Asia.

Dedication

You whom I could not save
Listen to me.
Try to understand this simple speech as I would be
    ashamed of another.
I swear, there is in me no wizardry of words.
I speak to you with silence like a cloud or a tree.

What strengthened me, for you was lethal.
You mixed up farewell to an epoch with the beginning
    of a new one,
Inspiration of hatred with lyrical beauty,
Blind force with accomplished shape.

Here is the valley of shallow Polish rivers. And an
    immense bridge
Going into white fog. Here is a broken city,
And the wind throws the screams of gulls on your grave
When I am talking with you.

What is poetry which does not save
Nations or people?
A connivance with official lies,
A song of drunkards whose throats will be cut in a
    moment,
Readings for sophomore girls.
That I wanted good poetry without knowing it,
That I discovered, late, its salutary aim,
In this and only this I find salvation.

They used to pour millet on graves or poppy seeds
To feed the dead who would come disguised as birds.
I put this book here for you, who once lived
So that you should visit us no more.

translated from the Polish by the author

The Colonel

What you have heard is true. I was in his house. His wife
carried a tray of coffee and sugar. His daughter filed her
nails, his son went out for the night. There were daily
papers, pet dogs, a pistol on the cushion beside him. The
moon swung bare on its black cord over the house. On the
television was a cop show. It was in English. Broken bottles
were embedded in the walls around the house to scoop the
kneecaps from a man's legs or cut his hands to lace. On the
windows there were gratings like those in liquor stores.
We had dinner, rack of lamb, good wine, a gold bell was on
the table for calling the maid. The maid brought green
mangoes, salt, a type of bread. I was asked how I enjoyed
the country. There was a brief commercial in Spanish. His
wife took everything away. There was some talk then of
how difficult it had become to govern. The parrot said hello
on the terrace. The colonel told it to shut up, and pushed
himself from the table. My friend said to me with his eyes:
say nothing. The colonel returned with a sack used to bring
groceries home. He spilled many human ears on the table.
They were like dried peach halves. There is no other way
to say this. He took one of them in his hands, shook it in
our faces, dropped it into a water glass. It came alive there.
I am tired of fooling around he said. As for the rights of any-
one, tell your people they can go fuck themselves. He swept
the ears to the floor with his arm and held the last of his
wine in the air. Something for your poetry, no? he said.
Some of the ears on the floor caught this scrap of his voice.
Some of the ears on the floor were pressed to the ground.

SEIICHI NIIKUNI

Anti-War

反戦
又戦
又戦
又

反 = anti　戦 = war　又 = again

Raiders' Dawn

Softly the civilized
Centuries fall,
Paper on paper,
Peter on Paul.

And lovers walking
From the night –
Eternity's masters,
Slaves of Time –
Recognise only
The drifting white
Fall of small faces
In pits of lime.

Blue necklace left
On a charred chair
Tells that Beauty
Was startled there.

The Horses

Barely a twelvemonth after
The seven days war that put the world to sleep,
Late in the evening the strange horses came.
By then we had made our covenant with silence,
But in the first few days it was so still
We listened to our breathing and were afraid.
On the second day
The radios failed; we turned the knobs; no answer.
On the third day a warship passed us, heading north,
Dead bodies piled on the deck. On the sixth day
A plane plunged over us into the sea. Thereafter
Nothing. The radios dumb;
And still they stand in corners of our kitchens,
And stand, perhaps, turned on, in a million rooms
All over the world. But now if they should speak,
If on a sudden they should speak again,
If on the stroke of noon a voice should speak,
We would not listen, we would not let it bring
That old bad world that swallowed its children quick
At one great gulp. We would not have it again.
Sometimes we think of the nations lying asleep,
Curled blindly in impenetrable sorrow,
And then the thought confounds us with its strangeness.

The tractors lie about our fields; at evening
They look like dank sea-monsters couched and waiting.
We leave them where they are and let them rust:
'They'll moulder away and be like other loam'.
We make our oxen drag our rusty ploughs,
Long laid aside. We have gone back

Far past our fathers' land.
                              And then, that evening
Late in the summer the strange horses came.
We heard a distant tapping on the road,
A deepening drumming; it stopped, went on again
And at the corner changed to hollow thunder.
We saw the heads
Like a wild wave charging and were afraid.
We had sold our horses in our fathers' time
To buy new tractors. Now they were strange to us
As fabulous steeds set on an ancient shield
Or illustrations in a book of knights.
We did not dare go near them. Yet they waited,
Stubborn and shy, as if they had been sent
By an old command to find our whereabouts
And that long-lost archaic companionship.
In the first moment we had never a thought
That they were creatures to be owned and used.
Among them were some half-a-dozen colts
Dropped in some wilderness of the broken world,
Yet new as if they had come from their own Eden.
Since then they have pulled our ploughs and borne our
    loads,
But that free servitude still can pierce our hearts.
Our life is changed; their coming our beginning.

Futility

Move him into the sun –
Gently its touch awoke him once,
At home, whispering of fields half-sown.
Always it woke him, even in France,
Until this morning and this snow.
If anything might rouse him now
The kind old sun will know.

Think how it wakes the seeds –
Woke once the clays of a cold star.
Are limbs, so dear achieved, are sides
Full-nerved, still warm, too hard to stir?
Was it for this the clay grew tall?
– O what made fatuous sunbeams toil
To break earth's sleep at all?

Green Beret

He was twelve years old,
and I do not know his name.
The mercenaries took him and his father,
whose name I do not know,
One morning upon the High Plateau.
Green Beret looked down on the frail boy
with the eyes of a hurt animal and thought,
a good fright will make him talk.
He commanded, and the father was taken away
behind the forest's green wall.
'Right kid tell us where they are,
tell us where or your father – dead.'
With eyes now bright and filled with terror
the slight boy said nothing.
'You've got one minute kid', said Green Beret,
'tell us where or we kill father'
and thrust his wrist-watch against a face all eyes,
the second-hand turning, jerking on its way.
'OK boy ten seconds to tell us where they are.'
In the last instant the silver hand shattered the
sky and the forest of trees.
'Kill the old guy' roared Green Beret
and shots hammered out
behind the forest's green wall
and sky and trees and soldiers stood,
in silence, and the boy cried out.
Green Beret stood
in silence, as the boy crouched down
and shook with tears,
as children do when their father dies.

'Christ,' said one mercenary to Green Beret,
'he didn't know a damn thing
we killed the old guy for nothing.'
So they all went away,
Green Beret and his mercenaries.

And the boy knew everything.
He knew everything about them, the caves,
the trails, the hidden places and the names,
and in the moment that he cried out,
in that same instant,
protected by frail tears
far stronger than any wall of steel,
they passed everywhere
like tigers
across the High Plateau.

translated from the Vietnamese

Essential Serbo-Croat

Guraj	Push
Pomozi mi	Help me
Boli	It hurts
Boli me	I have a pain
Boli me ovdje	I have a pain here
Bole me grudi	I have a pain in my breast
Bole me prsa	I have a pain in my chest
Boli me oko	I have a pain in my eye
Boli me stopalo	I have a pain in my foot
Boli me glava	I have a pain in my head
Hitno je	It's urgent
Ozbiljno je	It's serious
Boli me ovdje	It hurts here
Boli puno	It hurts a lot
To je jaka bol	It's a sharp pain
To je tupa bol	It's a dull pain
To je uporna bol	It's a nagging pain
Večinom vremena	Most of the time
Vrti mi se u glavi	I feel dizzy
Zlo mi je	I feel sick
Slabo mi je	I feel weak
Nije dobro	It's no good
Izgubio sam sve	I have lost everything
Ne mogu vam pomoči	I can't help you

American Football

(A Reflection upon the Gulf War)

Hallelullah!
It works.
We blew the shit out of them.

We blew the shit right back up their own ass
And out their fucking ears.

It works.
We blew the shit out of them.
They suffocated in their own shit!

Hallelullah.
Praise the Lord for all good things.

We blew them into fucking shit.
They are eating it.

Praise the Lord for all good things.

We blew their balls into shards of dust,
Into shards of fucking dust.

We did it.

Now I want you to come over here and kiss
    me on the mouth.

WILLIAM STAFFORD

At the Bomb Testing Site

At noon in the desert a panting lizard
waited for history, its elbows tense,
watching the curve of a particular road
as if something might happen.

It was looking for something farther off
than people could see, an important scene
acted in stone for little selves
at the flute end of consequences.

There was just a continent without much on it
under a sky that never cared less.
Ready for a change, the elbows waited.
The hands gripped hard on the desert.

The Fly

She sat on a willow-trunk
watching
part of the battle of Crécy,
the shouts,
the gasps,
the groans,
the tramping and the tumbling.

During the fourteenth charge
of the French cavalry
she mated
with a brown-eyed male fly
from Vadincourt.

She rubbed her legs together
as she sat on a disembowelled horse
meditating
on the immortality of flies.

With relief she alighted
on the blue tongue
of the Duke of Clervaux.

When silence settled
and only the whisper of decay
softly circled the bodies

and only
a few arms and legs
still twitched jerkily under the trees,

she began to lay her eggs
on the single eye
of Johann Uhr,
the Royal Armourer.

And thus it was
that she was eaten by a swift
fleeing
from the fires of Estrées.

translated from the Czech by George Theiner

Vergissmeinnicht

Three weeks gone and the combatants gone
returning over the nightmare ground
we found the place again, and found
the soldier sprawling in the sun.

The frowning barrel of his gun
overshadowing. As we came on
that day, he hit my tank with one
like the entry of a demon.

Look. Here in the gunpit spoil
the dishonoured picture of his girl
who has put: *Steffi. Vergissmeinnicht*
in a copybook gothic script.

We see him almost with content,
abased, and seeming to have paid
and mocked at by his own equipment
that's hard and good when he's decayed.

But she would weep to see today
how on his skin the swart flies move;
the dust upon the paper eye
and the burst stomach like a cave.

For here the lover and killer are mingled
who had one body and one heart.
And death who had the soldier singled
has done the lover mortal hurt.

Waiting for the Barbarians

What are we waiting for, assembled in the forum?

   The barbarians are due here today.

Why isn't anything going on in the senate?
Why are the senators sitting there without legislating?

   Because the barbarians are coming today.
   What's the point of senators making laws now?
   Once the barbarians are here, they'll do the legislating.

Why did our emperor get up so early,
and why is he sitting enthroned at the city's main gate,
in state, wearing the crown?

   Because the barbarians are coming today
   and the emperor's waiting to receive their leader.
   He's even got a scroll to give him,
   loaded with titles, with imposing names.

Why have our two consuls and praetors come out today
wearing their embroidered, their scarlet togas?
Why have they put on bracelets with so many amethysts,
rings sparkling with magnificent emeralds?
Why are they carrying elegant canes
beautifully worked in silver and gold?

   Because the barbarians are coming today
   and things like that dazzle the barbarians.

Why don't our distinguished orators turn up as usual
to make their speeches, say what they have to say?

Because the barbarians are coming today
and they're bored by rhetoric and public speaking.

Why this sudden bewilderment, this confusion?
(How serious people's faces have become.)
Why are the streets and squares emptying so rapidly,
everyone going home lost in thought?

Because night has fallen and the barbarians haven't
come.
And some of our men just in from the border say
there are no barbarians any longer.

Now what's going to happen to us without barbarians?
Those people were a kind of solution.

translated from the Greek by Edmund Keeley and Philip Sherrard

Familial

The mother does knitting
The son fights the war
She finds this quite natural the mother
And the father what does he do the father?
He does business
His wife does knitting
His son the war
He business
He finds this quite natural the father
And the son and the son
What does the son find the son?
He finds absolutely nothing the son
His mother does knitting his father business he war
When he finishes the war
He'll go into business with his father
The war continues the mother continues she knits
The father continues he does business
The son is killed he continues no more
The father and the mother go to the graveyard
They find this quite natural the father and mother
Life continues life with knitting war business
Business war knitting war
Business business business
Life with the graveyard.

translated from the French by Lawrence Ferlinghetti

August 6, 1945

In the Enola Gay
five minutes before impact
he whistles a dry tune

Later he will say
that the whole blooming sky
went up like an apricot ice.
Later he will laugh and tremble
at such a surrender, for the eye
of his belly saw Marilyn's skirts
fly over her head for ever

On the river bank,
bees drizzle over
hot white rhododendrons

Later she will walk
the dust, a scarlet girl
with her whole stripped skin
at her heel, stuck like an old
shoe sole or mermaid's tail

Later she will lie down
in the flecked black ash
where the people are become
as lizards or salamanders
and, blinded, she will complain:
Mother you are late, so late

Later in dreams he will look
down shrieking and see

        ladybirds
        ladybirds

SAMUEL TAYLOR COLERIDGE

from Fears in Solitude

                Thankless too for peace,
(Peace long preserved by fleets and perilous seas)
Secure from actual warfare, we have loved
To swell the war-whoop, passionate for war!
Alas! for ages ignorant of all
Its ghastlier workings, (famine or blue plague,
Battle, or siege, or flight through wintry snows),
We, this whole people, have been clamorous
For war and bloodshed; animating sports,
The which we pay for as a thing to talk of,
Spectators and not combatants! No guess
Anticipative of a wrong unfelt,
No speculation on contingency,
However dim and vague, too vague and dim
To yield a justifying cause; and forth,
(Stuffed out with big preamble, holy names,
And adjurations of the God in Heaven,)
We send our mandates for the certain death
Of thousands and ten thousands! Boys and girls,
And women, that would groan to see a child
Pull off an insect's leg, all read of war,
The best amusement for our morning-meal!
The poor wretch, who has learnt his only prayers
From curses, who knows scarcely words enough
To ask a blessing from his Heavenly Father,
Becomes a fluent phraseman, absolute
And technical in victories and defeats,
And all our dainty terms for fratricide;
Terms which we trundle smoothly o'er our tongues
Like mere abstractions, empty sounds to which

We join no feeling and attach no form!
As if the soldier died without a wound;
As if the fibres of this godlike frame
Were gored without a pang; as if the wretch,
Who fell in battle, doing bloody deeds,
Passed off to Heaven, translated and not killed;
As though he had no wife to pine for him,
No God to judge him! Therefore, evil days
Are coming on us, O my countrymen!
And what if all-avenging Providence,
Strong and retributive, should make us know
The meaning of our words, force us to feel
The desolation and the agony
Of our fierce doings?

Women, Children, Babies, Cows, Cats

'It was at My Lai or Sonmy or something,
it was this afternoon . . . We had these orders,
we had all night to think about it –
we was to burn and kill, then there'd be nothing
standing, women, children, babies, cows, cats . . .
As soon as we hopped the choppers, we started shooting.
I remember . . . as we was coming up upon one area
in Pinkville, a man with a gun . . . running – this lady . . .
Lieutenant LaGuerre said, "Shoot her." I said,
"You shoot her, I don't want to shoot no lady."
She had one foot in the door . . . When I turned her,
there was this little one-month-year-old baby
I thought was her gun. It kind of cracked me up.'

If I Only Knew

If I only knew
On what your last look rested.
Was it a stone that had drunk
So many last looks that they fell
Blindly upon its blindness?

Or was it earth,
Enough to fill a shoe,
And black already
With so much parting
And with so much killing?

Or was it your last road
That brought you a farewell from all the roads
You had walked?

A puddle, a bit of shining metal,
Perhaps the buckle of your enemy's belt,
Or some other small augury
Of heaven?

Or did this earth,
Which lets no one depart unloved,
Send you a bird-sign through the air,
Reminding your soul that it quivered
In the torment of its burnt body?

translated from the German by Ruth and Matthew Mead

NNAMDI OLEBARA

A Warrior's Lament

Now on the battlefield
I know what faces me.
It is death; my death.
I do not hate those I fight;
It is their deeds I hate.
Those I am fighting for do not love me;
My death shall not grieve them,
Nor shall it bring them joy.
No law compels me to fight;
None has sent me out to fight
Except my deep love for my own.
My friends want me to desert the field,
That I may not perish in battle.
But they forget: A serpent
Does not attack a child before its mother's eyes.
It is true that my mother, my mother's offspring,
My friends, the beautiful girl I want to marry,
Are worrying themselves to death about me;
Still I shall not leave the battlefield
For the enemy to march them away before my eyes.
I have left home to live in the bush.
The hunting I do now is the shooting of fellow humans.
I have become a beast of the forest
That I may bring peace to my own.
I am in the midst of battle now.
Listen to what is resounding in the forest where I stand!
Kwaku-kwaku is our morning greeting;
Unudum! Unudum! the song of guns!
As it sounds and resounds I become uncaring about life,
And strum my gun like a guitar.

When all the gunfire stops
I lift up my head,
I laugh;
When I turn around
The companions of my morning meal
Have become corpses.
I know one day it will be my turn.
I have already seen my death.
One day I will lie like my friends who lie here.
Vultures, termites, and other creatures of the forest
Shall hold a conference on top of me.
My bones will lie scattered in the bush.
When some farmer clears the forest
He'll gather up my skull and bones,
When he burns the debris of the forest he'll burn me.
When crops grow they'll grow on my bones;
No maiden shall kiss my lips
For the earth, it is not kissed.
Thus my life shall come to an end.
And my companions and my kin,
They shall lift up their eyes forever,
Up the road at the horizon,
Looking for one that shall never return.
And the last we shall see of each other
Was before I departed for war.
The next time we set eyes on each other
Shall be in the land of rest.

translated from the Igbo by Chinweizu

To His Love

He's gone, and all our plans
   Are useless indeed.
We'll walk no more on Cotswold
   Where the sheep feed
   Quietly and take no heed.

His body that was so quick
   Is not as you
Knew it, on Severn river
   Under the blue
   Driving our small boat through.

You would not know him now . . .
   But still he died
Nobly, so cover him over
   With violets of pride
   Purple from Severn side.

Cover him, cover him soon!
   And with thick-set
Masses of memoried flowers –
   Hide that red wet
   Thing I must somehow forget.

Johnny, I Hardly Knew Ye

While going the road to sweet Athy,
    Hurroo! Hurroo!
While going the road to sweet Athy,
    Hurroo! Hurroo!
While going the road to sweet Athy,
A stick in my hand and a drop in my eye,
A doleful damsel I heard cry:
  'Och, Johnny, I hardly knew ye!
    With drums and guns and guns and drums,
      The enemy nearly slew ye!
      My darling dear, you look so queer,
    Och, Johnny, I hardly knew ye!

'Where are your eyes that looked so mild?
    Hurroo! Hurroo!
Where are your eyes that looked so mild?
    Hurroo! Hurroo!
Where are your eyes that looked so mild
When my poor heart you first beguiled?
Why did you run from me and the child?
  Och, Johnny, I hardly knew ye!

'Where are the legs with which you run?
    Hurroo! Hurroo!
Where are the legs with which you run?
    Hurroo! Hurroo!
Where are the legs with which you run,
When you went to carry a gun? –
Indeed your dancing days are done!
  Och, Johnny, I hardly knew ye!

'It grieved my heart to see you sail,
    Hurroo! Hurroo!
It grieved my heart to see you sail,
    Hurroo! Hurroo!
It grieved my heart to see you sail,
Though from my heart you took leg bail, –
Like a cod you're doubled up head and tail,
    Och, Johnny, I hardly knew ye!

'You haven't an arm and you haven't a leg,
    Hurroo! Hurroo!
You haven't an arm and you haven't a leg,
    Hurroo! Hurroo!
You haven't an arm and you haven't a leg,
You're an eyeless, noseless, chickenless egg:
You'll have to be put in a bowl to beg,
    Och, Johnny, I hardly knew ye!

'I'm happy for to see you home,
    Hurroo! Hurroo!
I'm happy for to see you home,
    Hurroo! Hurroo!
I'm happy for to see you home,
All from the island of Sulloon,
So low in flesh, so high in bone,
    Och, Johnny, I hardly knew ye!

'But sad as it is to see you so,
    Hurroo! Hurroo!
But sad as it is to see you so,
    Hurroo! Hurroo!
But sad as it is to see you so,
And to think of you now as an object of woe,
Your Peggy'll still keep ye on as her beau.
    Och, Johnny, I hardly knew ye!

With drums and guns and guns and drums,
  The enemy nearly slew ye,
  My darling dear, you look so queer,
Och, Johnny, I hardly knew ye!'

NICCOLÒ DEGLI ALBIZZI

Prolonged Sonnet:
When the Troops were Returning from Milan

If you could see, fair brother, how dead beat
   The fellows look who come through Rome today, –
   Black yellow smoke-dried visages, – you'd say
They thought their haste at going all too fleet.
Their empty victual-waggons up the street
   Over the bridge dreadfully sound and sway;
   Their eyes, as hang'd men's, turning the wrong way;
And nothing on their backs, or heads, or feet.
One sees the ribs and all the skeletons
   Of their gaunt horses; and a sorry sight
Are the torn saddles, cramm'd with straw and stones.
   They are ashamed, and march throughout the night;
Stumbling, for hunger, on their marrowbones;
   Like barrels rolling, jolting, in this plight.
Their arms all gone, not even their swords are saved;
And each as silent as a man being shaved.

translated from the Italian by Dante Gabriel Rossetti

my sweet old etcetera
aunt lucy during the recent

war could and what
is more did tell you just
what everybody was fighting

for,
my sister

isabel created hundreds
(and
hundreds)of socks not to
mention shirts fleaproof earwarmers

etcetera wristers etcetera, my
mother hoped that

i would die etcetera
bravely of course my father used
to become hoarse talking about how it was
a privilege and if only he
could meanwhile my

self etcetera lay quietly
in the deep mud et

cetera
(dreaming,
et
    cetera, of
Your smile
eyes knees and of your Etcetera)

W. B. YEATS

On Being Asked for a War Poem

I think it better that in times like these
A poet's mouth be silent, for in truth
We have no gift to set a statesman right;
He has had enough of meddling who can please
A young girl in the indolence of her youth,
Or an old man upon a winter's night.

Seaman, 1941

This was not to be expected.

Waves, wind, and tide brought him again
to Barra. Clinging to driftwood many hours
the night before, he had not recognised
the current far off-shore his own nor
known he drifted home. He gave up, anyway,
some time before the smell of land reached out
or dawn outlined the morning gulls.

                    They found him
on the white sand southward of the ness,
not long enough in the sea to be
disfigured, cheek sideways as in sleep,
old men who had fished with his father
and grandfather and knew him at once,
before they even turned him on his back, by the set
of the dead shoulders, and were shocked.

This was not to be expected.

His mother, with hot eyes, preparing the parlour
for his corpse, would have preferred, she thought,
to have been told by telegram rather
than so to know that convoy, ship, and son
had only been a hundred miles north-west
of home when the torpedoes struck.
She could have gone on thinking that
he'd had no chance; but to die offshore,
in Hebridean tides, as if he'd stayed
a fisherman for life and never gone to war
was not to be expected.

BERTOLT BRECHT

War Has Been Given a Bad Name

I am told that the best people have begun saying
How, from a moral point of view, the Second World War
Fell below the standard of the First. The Wehrmacht
Allegedly deplores the methods by which the SS effected
The extermination of certain peoples. The Ruhr
   industrialists
Are said to regret the bloody manhunts
Which filled their mines and factories with slave workers.
   The intellectuals
So I heard, condemn industry's demand for slave workers
Likewise their unfair treatment. Even the bishops
Dissociate themselves from this way of waging war;
   in short the feeling
Prevails in every quarter that the Nazis did the Fatherland
A lamentably bad turn, and that war
While in itself natural and necessary, has, thanks to the
Unduly uninhibited and positively inhuman
Way in which it was conducted on this occasion, been
Discredited for some time to come.

translated from the German by John Willett

Channel Firing

That night your great guns, unawares,
Shook all our coffins as we lay,
And broke the chancel window-squares,
We thought it was the Judgment-day

And sat upright. While drearisome
Arose the howl of wakened hounds:
The mouse let fall the altar-crumb,
The worms drew back into the mounds,

The glebe cow drooled. Till God called, 'No;
It's gunnery practice out at sea
Just as before you went below;
The world is as it used to be:

'All nations striving strong to make
Red war yet redder. Mad as hatters
They do no more for Christés sake
Than you who are helpless in such matters.

'That this is not the judgment-hour
For some of them's a blessed thing,
For if it were they'd have to scour
Hell's floor for so much threatening . . .

'Ha, ha. It will be warmer when
I blow the trumpet (if indeed
I ever do; for you are men,
And rest eternal sorely need).'

So down we lay again. 'I wonder,
Will the world ever saner be,'
Said one, 'than when He sent us under
In our indifferent century!'

And many a skeleton shook his head.
'Instead of preaching forty year,'
My neighbour Parson Thirdly said,
'I wish I had stuck to pipes and beer.'

Again the guns disturbed the hour,
Roaring their readiness to avenge,
As far inland as Stourton Tower,
And Camelot, and starlit Stonehenge.

My Triumph lasted till the Drums
Had left the Dead alone
And then I dropped my Victory
And chastened stole along
To where the finished Faces
Conclusion turned on me
And then I hated Glory
And wished myself were They.

What is to be is best descried
When it has also been –
Could Prospect taste of Retrospect
The tyrannies of Men
Were Tenderer – diviner
The Transitive toward.
A Bayonet's contrition
Is nothing to the Dead.

from Hugh Selwyn Mauberley

These fought in any case,
and some believing,
> pro domo, in any case . . .

Some quick to arm,
some for adventure,
some from fear of weakness,
some from fear of censure,
some for love of slaughter, in imagination,
learning later . . .
some in fear, learning love of slaughter;
Died some, pro patria,
> non 'dulce' non 'et decor' . . .
walked eye-deep in hell
believing in old men's lies, then unbelieving
came home, home to a lie,
home to many deceits,
home to old lies and new infamy;
usury age-old and age-thick
and liars in public places.

Daring as never before, wastage as never before.
Young blood and high blood,
fair cheeks, and fine bodies;

fortitude as never before

frankness as never before,
disillusions as never told in the old days,

hysterias, trench confessions,
laughter out of dead bellies.

*

There died a myriad,
And of the best, among them,
For an old bitch gone in the teeth,
For a botched civilisation,

Charm, smiling at the good mouth,
Quick eyes gone under earth's lid,

For two gross of broken statues,
For a few thousand battered books.

EDWARD THOMAS

In Memoriam (Easter 1915)

The flowers left thick at nightfall in the wood
This Eastertide call into mind the men,
Now far from home, who, with their sweethearts, should
Have gathered them and will do never again.

Death Valley

Some Nazi or other has said that the Führer had restored
to German manhood the 'right and joy of dying in battle'.

Sitting dead in Death Valley
below Ruweisat Ridge
a boy with his forelock down about his cheek
and his face slate-grey.

I thought of the right and the joy
that he got from his Führer,
of falling in the field of slaughter
to rise no more;

of the pomp and the fame
that he had, not alone,
though he was the most piteous to see
in a valley gone to seed

with flies about grey corpses
on a dun sand
dirty yellow and full of the rubbish
and fragments of battle.

Was the boy of the band
who abused the Jews
and Communists, or of the greater
band of those

led, from the beginning of generations,
unwillingly to the trial
and mad delirium of every war
for the sake of rulers?

Whatever his desire or mishap,
his innocence or malignity,
he showed no pleasure in his death
below Ruweisat Ridge.

Suicide in the Trenches

I knew a simple soldier boy
Who grinned at life in empty joy,
Slept soundly through the lonesome dark,
And whistled early with the lark.

In winter trenches, cowed and glum,
With crumps and lice and lack of rum,
He put a bullet through his brain.
No one spoke of him again.

.   .   .

You smug-faced crowds with kindling eye
Who cheer when soldier lads march by,
Sneak home and pray you'll never know
The hell where youth and laughter go.

Testimony

'We were killing pigs when the Yanks arrived.
A Tuesday morning, sunlight and gutter-blood
Outside the slaughter house. From the main road
They would have heard the screaming,
Then heard it stop and had a view of us
In our gloves and aprons coming down the hill.
Two lines of them, guns on their shoulders, marching.
Armoured cars and tanks and open jeeps.
Sunburnt hands and arms. Unnamed, in step,
Hosting for Normandy.
                              Not that we knew then
Where they were headed, standing there like youngsters
As they tossed us gum and tubes of coloured sweets.'

Facing It

My black face fades,
hiding inside the black granite.
I said I wouldn't,
dammit: No tears.
I'm stone. I'm flesh.
My clouded reflection eyes me
like a bird of prey, the profile of night
slanted against morning. I turn
this way – the stone lets me go.
I turn that way – I'm inside
the Vietnam Veterans Memorial
again, depending on the light
to make a difference.
I go down the 58,022 names,
half-expecting to find
my own in letters like smoke.
I touch the name Andrew Johnson;
I see the booby trap's white flash.
Names shimmer on a woman's blouse
but when she walks away
the names stay on the wall.
Brushstrokes flash, a red bird's
wings cutting across my stare.
The sky. A plane in the sky.
A white vet's image floats
closer to me, then his pale eyes
look through mine. I'm a window.
He's lost his right arm
inside the stone. In the black mirror

a woman's trying to erase names:
No, she's brushing a boy's hair.

Shiloh

A Requiem
(April 1862)

Skimming lightly, wheeling still,
  The swallows fly low
Over the field in clouded days,
  The forest-field of Shiloh –
Over the field where April rain
Solaced the parched ones stretched in pain
Through the pause of night
That followed the Sunday fight
  Around the church of Shiloh –
The church so lone, the log-built one,
That echoed to many a parting groan
    And natural prayer
  Of dying foemen mingled there –
Foemen at morn, but friends at eve –
  Fame or country least their care:
(What like a bullet can undeceive!)
  But now they lie low,
While over them the swallows skim,
  And all is hushed at Shiloh.

In one of the bloodiest battles of the American Civil War, 24,000 troops
died at Shiloh, Tennessee, 1862

RICHARD EBERHART

The Fury of Aerial Bombardment

You would think the fury of aerial bombardment
Would rouse God to relent; the infinite spaces
Are still silent. He looks on shock-pried faces.
History, even, does not know what is meant.

You would feel that after so many centuries
God would give man to repent; yet he can kill
As Cain could, but with multitudinous will,
No farther advanced than in his ancient furies.

Was man made stupid to see his own stupidity?
Is God by definition indifferent, beyond us all?
Is the eternal truth man's fighting soul
Wherein the Beast ravens in its own avidity?

Of Van Wettering I speak, and Averill,
Names on a list, whose faces I do not recall
But they are gone to early death, who late in school
Distinguished the belt feed lever from the belt holding
  pawl.

from Amours de Voyage, Canto II

Dulce it is, and *decorum*, no doubt, for the country to fall,
  – to
Offer one's blood an oblation to Freedom, and die for the
  Cause; yet
Still, individual culture is also something, and no man
Finds quite distinct the assurance that he of all others is
  called on,
Or would be justified even, in taking away from the world
  that
Precious creature, himself. Nature sent him here to abide
  here;
Else why send him at all? Nature wants him still, it is
  likely;
On the whole, we are meant to look after ourselves; it is
  certain
Each has to eat for himself, digest for himself, and in
  general
Care for his own dear life, and see to his own preservation;
Nature's intentions, in most things uncertain, in this are
  decisive;
Which, on the whole, I conjecture the Romans will follow,
  and I shall.
So we cling to our rocks like limpets; Ocean may bluster,
Over and under and round us; we open our shells to
  imbibe our
Nourishment, close them again, and are safe, fulfilling the
  purpose
Nature intended, – a wise one, of course, and a noble,
  we doubt not.

Sweet it may be and decorous, perhaps, for the country
  to die; but,
On the whole, we conclude the Romans won't do it, and
  I sha'n't.

Arthur Hugh Clough witnessed the Siege of Rome in 1849

MCMXIV

Those long uneven lines
Standing as patiently
As if they were stretched outside
The Oval or Villa Park,
The crowns of hats, the sun
On moustached archaic faces
Grinning as if it were all
An August Bank Holiday lark;

And the shut shops, the bleached
Established names on the sunblinds,
The farthings and sovereigns,
And dark-clothed children at play
Called after kings and queens,
The tin advertisements
For cocoa and twist, and the pubs
Wide open all day;

And the countryside not caring:
The place-names all hazed over
With flowering grasses, and fields
Shadowing Domesday lines
Under wheat's restless silence;
The differently-dressed servants
With tiny rooms in huge houses,
The dust behind limousines;

Never such innocence,
Never before or since,
As changed itself to past
Without a word – the men

Leaving the gardens tidy,
The thousands of marriages
Lasting a little while longer:
Never such innocence again.

Wounds

Here are two pictures fom my father's head –
I have kept them like secrets until now:
First, the Ulster Division at the Somme
Going over the top with 'Fuck the Pope!'
'No Surrender!': a boy about to die,
Screaming 'Give 'em one for the Shankill!'
'Wilder than Gurkhas' were my father's words
Of admiration and bewilderment.
Next comes the London-Scottish padre
Resettling kilts with his swagger-stick.
With a stylish backhand and a prayer.
Over a landscape of dead buttocks
My father followed him for fifty years.
At last, a belated casualty,
He said – lead traces flaring till they hurt –
'I am dying for King and Country, slowly.'
I touched his hand, his thin head I touched.

Now, with military honours of a kind,
With his badges, his medals like rainbows,
His spinning compass, I bury beside him
Three teenage soldiers, bellies full of
Bullets and Irish beer, their flies undone.
A packet of Woodbines I throw in,
A lucifer, the Sacred Heart of Jesus
Paralysed as heavy guns put out
The night-light in a nursery for ever;
Also a bus-conductor's uniform –
He collapsed beside his carpet-slippers
Without a murmur, shot through the head

By a shivering boy who wandered in
Before they could turn the television down
Or tidy away the supper dishes.
To the children, to a bewildered wife,
I think 'Sorry Missus' was what he said.

Shemà

You who live secure
In your warm houses,
Who return at evening to find
Hot food and friendly faces:

> Consider whether this is a man,
> Who labors in the mud
> Who knows no peace
> Who fights for a crust of bread
> Who dies at a yes or a no.
> Consider whether this is a woman,
> Without hair or name
> With no more strength to remember
> Eyes empty and womb cold
> As a frog in winter.

Consider that this has been:
I commend these words to you.
Engrave them on your hearts
When you are in your house, when you walk
    on your way,
When you go to bed, when you rise.
Repeat them to your children.
Or may your house crumble,
Disease render you powerless,
Your offspring avert their faces from you.

translated from the Italian by Ruth Feldman and Brian Stone

September 1, 1939

I sit in one of the dives
On Fifty-Second Street
Uncertain and afraid
As the clever hopes expire
Of a low dishonest decade:
Waves of anger and fear
Circulate over the bright
And darkened lands of the earth,
Obsessing our private lives;
The unmentionable odour of death
Offends the September night.

Accurate scholarship can
Unearth the whole offence
From Luther until now
That has driven a culture mad,
Find what occurred at Linz,
What huge imago made
A psychopathic god:
I and the public know
What all schoolchildren learn,
Those to whom evil is done
Do evil in return.

Exiled Thucydides knew
All that a speech can say
About Democracy,
And what dictators do,
The elderly rubbish they talk
To an apathetic grave;

Analysed all in his book,
The enlightenment driven away,
The habit-forming pain,
Mismanagement and grief:
We must suffer them all again.

Into this neutral air
Where blind skyscrapers use
Their full height to proclaim
The strength of Collective Man,
Each language pours its vain
Competitive excuse:
But who can live for long
In an euphoric dream;
Out of the mirror they stare,
Imperialism's face
And the international wrong.

Faces along the bar
Cling to their average day:
The lights must never go out,
The music must always play,
All the conventions conspire
To make this fort assume
The furniture of home;
Lest we should see where we are,
Lost in a haunted wood,
Children afraid of the night
Who have never been happy or good.

The windiest militant trash
Important Persons shout
Is not so crude as our wish:
What mad Nijinsky wrote
About Diaghilev

Is true of the normal heart;
For the error bred in the bone
Of each woman and each man
Craves what it cannot have,
Not universal love
But to be loved alone.

From the conservative dark
Into the ethical life
The dense commuters come,
Repeating their morning vow,
'I *will* be true to the wife,
I'll concentrate more on my work',
And helpless governors wake
To resume their compulsory game:
Who can release them now,
Who can reach the deaf,
Who can speak for the dumb?

All I have is a voice
To undo the folded lie,
The romantic lie in the brain
Of the sensual man-in-the-street
And the lie of Authority
Whose buildings grope the sky:
There is no such thing as the State
And no one exists alone;
Hunger allows no choice
To the citizen or the police;
We must love one another or die.

Defenceless under the night
Our world in stupor lies;
Yet, dotted everywhere,
Ironic points of light

Flash out wherever the Just
Exchange their messages:
May I, composed like them
Of Eros and of dust,
Beleaguered by the same
Negation and despair,
Show an affirming flame.

ISAAC ROSENBERG

August 1914

What in our lives is burnt
In the fire of this?
The heart's dear granary?
The much we shall miss?

Three lives hath one life –
Iron, honey, gold.
The gold, the honey gone –
Left is the hard and cold.

Iron are our lives
Molten right through our youth.
A burnt space through ripe fields
A fair mouth's broken tooth.

History

St Andrews: West Sands; September 2001

Today
     as we flew the kites
– the sand spinning off in ribbons along the beach
and that gasoline smell from Leuchars gusting across
the golf links;
        the tide far out
and quail-grey in the distance;
             people
jogging, or stopping to watch
as the war planes cambered and turned
in the morning light –

today
     – with the news in my mind, and the muffled dread
of what may come –

          I knelt down in the sand
with Lucas
     gathering shells
and pebbles
     finding evidence of life in all this
driftwork:
     snail shells; shreds of razorfish;
smudges of weed and flesh on tideworn stone.

At times I think what makes us who we are
is neither kinship nor our given states
but something lost between the world we own
and what we dream about behind the names

on days like this
                    our lines raised in the wind
our bodies fixed and anchored to the shore

and though we are confined by property
what tethers us to gravity and light
has most to do with distance and the shapes
we find in water
                    reading from the book
of silt and tides
                    the rose or petrol blue
of jellyfish and sea anemone
combining with a child's
first nakedness.

Sometimes I am dizzy with the fear
of losing everything – the sea, the sky,
all living creatures, forests, estuaries:
we trade so much to know the virtual
we scarcely register the drift and tug
of other bodies
                    scarcely apprehend
the moment as it happens: shifts of light
and weather
                    and the quiet, local forms
of history: the fish lodged in the tide
beyond the sands;
                    the long insomnia
of ornamental carp in public parks
captive and bright
                    and hung in their own
slow-burning
              transitive gold;
                              jamjars of spawn

and sticklebacks
                    or goldfish carried home
from fairgrounds
                    to the hum of radio

but this is the problem: how to be alive
in all this gazed-upon and cherished world
and do no harm

                    a toddler on a beach
sifting wood and dried weed from the sand
and puzzled by the pattern on a shell

his parents on the dune slacks with a kite
plugged into the sky
                    all nerve and line

patient; afraid; but still, through everything
attentive to the irredeemable.

Night in Al-Hamra

A candle on the long road
A candle in the slumbering houses
A candle for the terrified stores
A candle for the bakeries
A candle for the journalist shuddering in an
  empty office
A candle for the fighter
A candle for the doctor at the sick bed
A candle for the wounded
A candle for honest talk
A candle for staircases
A candle for the hotel crowded with refugees
A candle for the singer
A candle for the broadcasters in a shelter
A candle for a bottle of water
A candle for the air
A candle for two lovers in a stripped apartment
A candle for the sky that has folded
A candle for the beginning
A candle for the end
A candle for the final decision
A candle for conscience
A candle in my hand

translated from the Arabic by Khaled Mattawa

Afterword

For centuries there was no such thing as a 'war poet' in the modern sense of the phrase. Poets wrote about war as they did about any other subject – from a variety of angles, and with a wide range of attitudes. Ancient Greeks and Romans extolled the victories of the state, the courage of soldiers, the brilliance of leaders, the making of heroes. Old English and Norse poets accepted loss as something unavoidable in the struggle for survival and reputation – Beowulf, for instance, is described as 'the man most gracious and fair-minded, / Kindest to his people and keenest to win fame'. Shakespeare, for all his compassion, recognised that war had sometimes been necessary to define and stabilise the Elizabethan crown. This is not to say pre-modern poets were oblivious to suffering: to recognise this, we only have to read Chaucer writing about the Hundred Years War with France (1337–1453), or Coleridge writing about the fears of invasion in 1798, or Whitman writing about the American Civil War in the 1860s. But sympathy, fear, dismay and sorrow do not form the whole of the story, as this anthology proves. Its disparate voices also celebrate, honour, prize and endorse.

But the book also proves something else. Towards the end of the First World War, amidst the squalor and tragedy of the Western Front, something fundamental changed. Wilfred Owen, Siegfried Sassoon, Ivor Gurney and Isaac Rosenberg – along with less famous others – began writing in ways which not only questioned the purpose of war, but also challenged previous poetic orthodoxies. The patriotic imperative 'Dulce Et Decorum Est' became 'that old lie', and in the process our sense of 'a war poet' was transformed. 'This book', Wilfred Owen wrote about the collection of his poems that he did not live to see published, '[is not] about deeds, or lands, nor anything about glory, honour, might, majesty, dominion, or power'. Its subject was 'War and the pity of War'. It was still possible to celebrate individual acts of courage and to commemorate losses, but not to glorify conflict as such. 'All a poet can do today is warn,' Owen went on. 'That is why the true poets must be truthful.'

Owen's maxim has held firm through the years, even in wars (such as the war against Hitler) which are generally considered 'just'. The north-African poems of Keith Douglas, for instance, may take a seemingly insouciant attitude to battles, but they leave us in no doubt about war's misery and waste. The same thing applies even more obviously to later poems about the Holocaust, or Vietnam, or the Gulf War of 1991. 'Pity' and 'truthfulness' remain the crucial ingredients, even – or especially – when the realities of war are blurred by euphemisms ('friendly fire', 'collateral damage'), and by the strange separations of TV screens.

In certain respects this may seem to imply a narrowing: we can guess what attitude poets will take to a conflict before we read a line they have written about it. Which in turn suggests their poems will be confirmations rather than surprises. Yet in the modern war poems gathered here we continue to feel surprised, let alone shocked and appalled. This is because the best war poets *react* to their experience of war, rather than simply acting in response to its pressures. They are mindful of the larger peace-time context even when dwelling on particular horrors; they engage with civilian as well as military life; they impose order and personality as these things are threatened; they insist on performing acts of the imagination when faced with barbarism. In this respect, and in spite of its variety, their work makes a common plea for humanity.

This anthology would be significant whenever it were published. The fact that it appears now, with the world on red alert and the West threatening to invade Iraq, gives it a special value and poignancy. It reminds us that poetry reflects our strongest and truest feelings at moments of crisis. It brings us face to face with the terror of war at a time when our airwaves are filled with talk of the war on terror. It shows us that – whatever our faith – we compromise, betray or wreck our selves when we take up arms against one another.

ANDREW MOTION

Acknowledgements

The editors and publishers gratefully acknowledge permission to
reprint copyright material in this book as follows:

ARCHILOCHUS: to Oxford University Press, trans. © M. L. West,
Greek Lyric Poetry (1993). YEHUDA AMICHAI: to Faber & Faber Ltd,
trans. Yehuda Amichai and Ted Hughes, from *Selected Poems* (2000).
W. H. AUDEN: to Faber & Faber Ltd for 'O What is That Sound', from
Collected Poems (1981), and 'September 1, 1939', from *The English
Auden* (1977). HILAIRE BELLOC: to the Peters Fraser & Dunlop
Group Ltd, from *Complete Verse*. ELIZABETH BISHOP: to Chatto &
Windus, from *Complete Poems* (1991). EDMUND BLUNDEN: to
A. D. Peters & Co. Ltd. BERTOLT BRECHT: to Eyre Methuen, 'In Dark
Times' trans. © Humphrey Milnes, 'War Has Been Given a Bad Name'
trans. © John Willett, from *Poems 1913–1956* (1976). JOHN BURNSIDE:
to Random House UK Ltd, from *The Light Trap* (Cape, 2002).
HAYDEN CARRUTH: to Copper Canyon, from *Collected Shorter Poems
1946–1991* (1992). MICHAEL CASEY: copyright © 1989 by Michael
Casey, from *Obscenities* (1972), reprinted by permission of Carnegie
Mellon University Press. C. P. CAVAFY: to Random House UK Ltd,
trans. Edmund Keeley and Philip Sherrard, from *Collected Poems*, ed.
George Savidis (Chatto, 1990). E. E. CUMMINGS: to W. W. Norton &
Company Ltd, from *Complete Poems 1904–1962* by E. E. Cummings,
ed. George J. Firmage, copyright © 1931, 1959, 1979, 1991 by the
Trustees for the E. E. Cummings Trust and George James Firmage.
MAHMOUD DARWISH: trans. © Sarah Maguire, 2003. EMILY
DICKINSON: to Harvard University Press and the Trustees of
Amherst College, from *The Poems of Emily Dickinson*, ed. Thomas
Johnson, Mass.: The Belknap Press of Harvard University Press,
copyright © 1951, 1955, 1979, 1983 by the President and
Fellows of Harvard College. KEITH DOUGLAS: to Faber & Faber
Ltd, from *The Complete Poems of Keith Douglas*, ed. Desmond
Graham (1978). PAUL DURCAN: to The Harvill Press, from *A Snail
in My Prime* (1993). RICHARD EBERHART: to Chatto & Windus,
from *Collected Poems 1930–1976*. D. J. ENRIGHT: to Oxford

to Faber & Faber Ltd for 'Hugh Selwyn Mauberley' and 'Lament of the Frontier Guard', from *Collected Shorter Poems*. JACQUES PRÉVERT: trans. © 1958 Lawrence Ferlinghetti, from *Selections from 'Paroles'* (Penguin, 1965). SAMIH AL-QASIM: translation by Abdullah al-Udhari (ed.), *Modern Poetry of the Arab World*, (Harmondsworth: Penguin, 1986). ISAAC ROSENBERG: to Chatto & Windus Ltd, the Literary Estate of Isaac Rosenberg and Schocken Books for 'August 1914' and 'Break of Day in the Trenches', from *The Collected Works of Isaac Rosenberg*, ed. Ian Parsons. TADEUSZ RÓŻEWICZ: from *They Came to See a Poet*, trans. © Adam Czerniawski (Anvil, 1991). NELLY SACHS: to Penguin Books, trans. © Ruth and Matthew Mead, from *Selected Poems* (1971). CARL SANDBURG: to Harcourt Brace & Company, from *Cornhuskers* by Carl Sandburg, copyright 1918 by Holt, Rinehart & Winston Inc, and renewed 1946 by Carl Sandburg. SAPPHO: to Oxford University Press, trans. © M. L. West, *Greek Lyric Poetry* (1993). SIEGFRIED SASSOON: to Faber & Faber Ltd for 'The General' and 'Suicide in the Trenches', from *Collected Poems 1908–1956* (1984). JO SHAPCOTT: to Faber and Faber Ltd. GORAN SIMIĆ: copyright © David Harsent, from *Sprinting from the Graveyard* (OUP, 1997). KEN SMITH: to Bloodaxe Books, from *Shed* (2002). STEVIE SMITH: to the James MacGibbon Estate, from *Collected Poems*, ed. James MacGibbon (Penguin, 1985). WILLIAM STAFFORD: to Harper and Row, Publishers, Inc., from *Stories That Could be True*, © 1960 William Stafford. HO THIEN: to Heinemann Educational Publishers, from *Axed Between the Ears* by David Kitchen. DYLAN THOMAS: to David Higham Associates Ltd, from *The Poems of Dylan Thomas* (Dent, 1971). EDWARD THOMAS: to Faber & Faber Ltd, for 'In Memoriam' and 'Rain', from *Collected Poems*. MARINA TSVETAEVA: to Oxford University Press, trans. © Elaine Feinstein, from *Selected Poems* (1993). BRUCE WEIGL: from *Executioner* (Ironwood, 1976). JAMES WRIGHT: to Farrar, Straus & Giroux, Inc., from *Above the River* (1990). W. B. YEATS: to A. P. Watt Ltd on behalf of Michael B. Yeats, from *Poems*, ed. Richard J. Finneran (Macmillan, 1991). SAADI YOUSSEF: to Graywolf Press, trans. © Khaled Mattawa, from *Without An Alphabet, Without A Face* (2002).

Index of Poets and Translators

Index of First Lines

[145]